Baritone/Bass
CLASSICAL CONTEST SOLOS
With Companion Audio

CONTENTS

On the Recordings:
*Jan Jarvis, baritone
**Jeffrey Ray, baritone
Laura Ward, piano
Martha Gerhart, German and Italian language coach
Lelia Tenreyro, Spanish language coach

Recorded at WFMT studios, Chicago, 2/97
Larry Rock, engineer

To access companion recorded full performances,
piano accompaniments, and pronunciation lessons online, visit:
www.halleonard.com/mylibrary

4699-5661-6027-8311

ISBN 978-0-7935-7800-9

HAL•LEONARD®
CORPORATION
7777 W. BLUEMOUND RD. P.O. BOX 13819 MILWAUKEE, WI 53213

Visit Hal Leonard Online at
www.halleonard.com

LEARNING A SONG

What is an art song?

An art song is a composition, usually for voice and piano, of a classical nature. A composer chooses a poem or some prose and sets the words to music. This differs from popular songs, not only in musical style, but in artistic approach. For the genre of a popular song (anything from a song by George and Ira Gershwin to a song written by Sting) the words and music are written together. An art song is a musical reaction to an existing poem or text. The composer responds to the meaning of the words, as well as meanings that are implied, in a free, expressive manner. Art songs composed to poetry are a European tradition dating back to at least the Renaissance, and composers still continue to write new art songs today. The richest period for art song composition was in Germany, France and Italy during the nineteenth century. Many major composers created a large number of new art songs, for example, Schubert, Schumann, Fauré, Brahms, Mendelssohn, Wolf, Strauss, Bellini, Donaudy, and many others. Sometimes folksongs are arranged in an approach that gives them the sensibility of an art song intended for a singer and piano on the recital stage. Such is the case with Burleigh's settings of spirituals found in *Classical Contest Solos*.

Choosing a Song

The most important factor in your success in performing any song, whether it be an art song, a pop song, or a theater song, is choosing a song that is suitable for your voice. Deciding which song to sing will necessitate some experimentation when you are just beginning to study voice. Choose a song that you like. Make certain that the vocal range is reasonable for you. There probably will be some vocal challenges for you, and that is as it should be. Don't make the mistake of choosing a song that is so difficult for you that it becomes a burden, and is something that you ultimately cannot sing at your best. The songs in *Classical Contest Solos* vary some in vocal difficulty, but all should be reasonable for student singers. Nevertheless, they pose different challenges.

The Poem

Always remember that in art song the words came first. The composer's song wouldn't exist without the poet's original words, sometimes written hundreds of years before the song was composed. You will do well to begin your study of a song by first pondering the words. What do they mean? Is there an implied character that says the words? (Sometimes this is true, but not always.) What is implied, but left unsaid? Is there something that has happened before the poem begins? You will have to use your imagination and insight to arrive at your own conclusions. Is the language of the poem stylized in some way, because of the period in which it was written, or the nationality of the author, or because the author chose deliberately to say things in a particular way? What are the most important words in the poem? If you have difficulty understanding a poem you might ask for help from someone experienced in poetry and literature, an English teacher, for example.

As you ponder the poem's meaning you should recite the words aloud. An actor learning a part would naturally say the words aloud many times, experimenting with different inflections and stresses. A singer should work in the same way, considering the words of the song over and over from many different points of view. After you learn the music, which we will soon address, the crucial next step is to attempt to discover what the *composer* felt the poem is about, and how his/her setting of the words to music reveals the meaning. You may discover that the composer has interpreted the words in a way different from anything you had previously considered.

Songs in a Foreign Language

All of the comments in the section above also apply to a song for which the words are in Italian, German, Spanish, or any language other than English. Yet there is an obvious added challenge: You must learn to correctly pronounce a poem in a language that you probably do not speak. Classical singers the world over, particularly in the United States, learn early on that they must be proficient in singing in the major European languages. This does not mean that they all can speak these languages fluently.

Why do we not just translate art songs originally written in German, Italian, Spanish, French, or any other language into English? The answer is that the original poem is so intricately a part of the music that changing the words in any way would be the same as altering the music. It is also very difficult, if not impossible, to adequately translate a poem into another language and retain the subtleties of meanings originally intended. The English translations in *Classical Contest Solos* are for comprehension and study, but they are not designed to be sung. In opera it may make sense sometimes to translate the words for an audience sitting in the theater trying to follow a plot. But art song is a far more intimate kind of composition. It is generally accepted internationally that, with rare exceptions, an art song always should be performed in the original language.

The recorded pronunciation lessons on the companion audio will aid you greatly in learning how to pronounce the words to a poem in a foreign language. This study must be very meticulous. Do not just approximate the sounds you hear by the recorded teacher. Work at exactly imitating the vowels and consonants. Once you can accurately pronounce the text of the poem phonetically, practice speaking it many times until it becomes a fluent expression. Put the poems in your own words to discover the meanings. Your goal is for those who hear you sing the song to believe that you are a fluent, native speaker of the language you sing. Does that sound impossible? It isn't, with hard, intelligent work.

Learning the Melody and Rhythms

After you have studied the words as described above, which may take several days of study, it is time to learn the musical notes. If you are capable of playing an instrument, you will do best to play a phrase, then sing it as you study the notes. Repeat the phrase as many times as is necessary for you to feel you know all the notes and rhythms correctly. If you do not play an instrument, and many singers do not, you may want to consider taking piano lessons. This will help enormously. In the meantime, you will have to ask someone to play the melody notes for you. Listen carefully to the pitches and rhythms, and practice them regularly until you know them completely. It is very important that you also learn how many beats of rest there are whenever you are not singing. Many singers fail to study rests carefully, and the result is that they enter early with a vocal phrase, or are late in coming in at the correct spot.

The companion recording can help you to learn a song. Listen carefully to the singer on the recording, all the while following along, studying the notes on the page. You can stop the recording and study a phrase at a time like this. One word of caution: While it may be very useful for you to use the recording to learn the notes, you will not want to imitate every interpretive nuance as done by the recorded singer. You will want to study the song thoroughly so that you can come up with your own interpretation.

Practice

After you have studied the words and learned the melody and rhythms, you must practice the song regularly, probably meaning almost every single day. Remember that classical singing is not just about getting the pronunciation, notes and rhythms right. You must work on your singing, learning how to produce the most beautiful and natural sound possible, smoothly moving from one note to the next. This is best accomplished with the guidance of a voice teacher. However, you might ask your choral director for help, or your church choir director. Practice sessions should begin with warm-ups. Remember that beautiful classical singing is never strained. Do not try to make more sound than is naturally comfortable. Your aim is a healthy, open sound that is supported by good breathing. The ultimate aim is to have no tension in your jaw, your throat, your face, or anywhere else in your body as you sing. A solid, low breath from the diaphragm (in the abdomen) is absolutely necessary, not a high, shallow breath that comes from your chest. The recorded accompaniments on the companion audio will help you greatly in your practice. However, when you perform a song with a live pianist you are free to take a different tempo than the one on the recording.

Memorizing

All songs that solo singers present in a performance with piano should be memorized. College voice majors sing a whole recital from memory. Professional artists sing a repertoire of many opera roles in several languages, all from memory. If you are having difficulty memorizing a song, it is probably because you haven't studied it long enough or carefully enough.

Performing

You should find ways to get your nerves under control. Practice "performing" for your friends or family before you sing for judges or an audience. You should know the music *extremely well.* All too often students quickly learn a song the week before a performance, then don't quite understand when things don't go smoothly. You should know something very well several weeks before the performance. Only then will you be able to express yourself as an emerging artist, communicating something from within you. In the best situation you will perform with a pianist, not with the recorded practice accompaniment.

Adela

Una muchacha guapa,	*A nice looking girl,*
llamada Adela,	*named Adela,*
los amores de Juan	*whose love for Juan*
la lleva enferma,	*is making her ill,*
y ella sabía,	*and she knew*
que su amiga Dolores	*that her friend Dolores*
lo entretenía.	*entertained him.*

JOAQUÍN RODRIGO (1901–1999)

Spanish composer Joaquín Rodrigo was only three years old when he suffered the permanent loss of his sight. His parents, realizing the young boy's natural musical ability, sought out the best music teachers available. Eventually Rodrigo was sent to Paris where he became a student of Paul Dukas at the prestigious École Normale de Musique. It was in Paris that he met fellow Spaniard Manuel de Falla. Some 26 years older than Rodrigo, de Falla was encouraging to his young colleague. Rodrigo returned to Spain in 1939, following the Spanish Civil War. After the terrifically successful premiere of his Concerto de Aranjuez, in 1940, he was hailed as Spain's leading composer. In 1944 he was appointed as music advisor to Spanish Radio, followed two years later by his appointment to the Manuel de Falla Chair at the University of Madrid, a position that was created expressly for him. In addition to several stage works, Rodrigo composed several concertos for various instruments, a number of songs and quite a few small instrumental works, many of which feature guitar.

THOUGHTS ABOUT THE SONG ...

This is a very characteristic Spanish ballad composed to an anonymous folk text. Songs in this style typically have simple words that contain strong emotion. In "Adela" it's easy to hear a guitar in the piano accompaniment. One can imagine a Spanish singer in a sleepy tavern singing this sad song as he plays his guitar. With a tangible situation like the one this song portrays, it's best to try and imagine everything you can about Adela's story. Here's one possible scenario (you may come up with another version of your own). Try and picture this sad young woman, actually becoming physically ill from heartache. She loved Juan with all her heart, and thought he loved her. She had imagined their lives together, being married, having a home and children together. Then one day she somehow discovers that Juan has been seeing her good friend Dolores. Adela has been betrayed by the two people she loves best in the world, and feels completely alone. She awakens each day to the same despair. It never leaves her. She can't bring herself to smile at anyone, and only speaks when necessary. This is the sadness you describe in this brief song. Attempt to find some spontaneity as you tell her story to an audience. If Spanish is not a principal language to you, you will need to work with the companion recording on your pronunciation. Perfect your pronunciation, speaking the words over and over, until you feel they are completely fluent, and that you are able to express emotion with them. This may take several days of work. Only at that point should you begin to sing the words.

PRONUNCIATION TIPS

Joaquín [yo-ah-**keen**] Rodrigo [rohd-**ree**-goh]

Adela

Anonymous Spanish poem

music by
Joaquín Rodrigo

Andantino

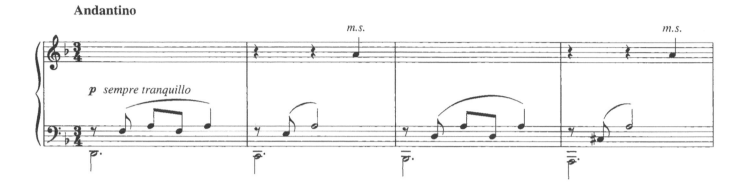

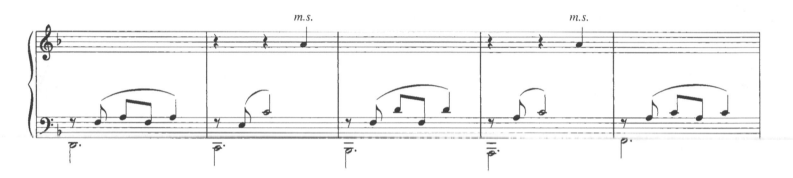

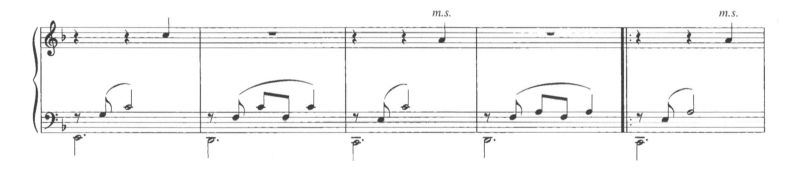

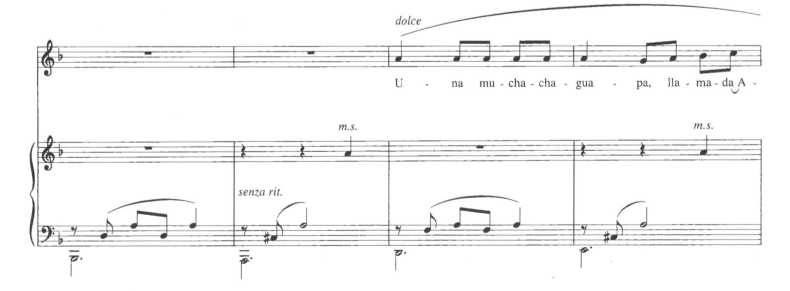

U – na mu – cha – cha gua – pa, lla – ma – da A –

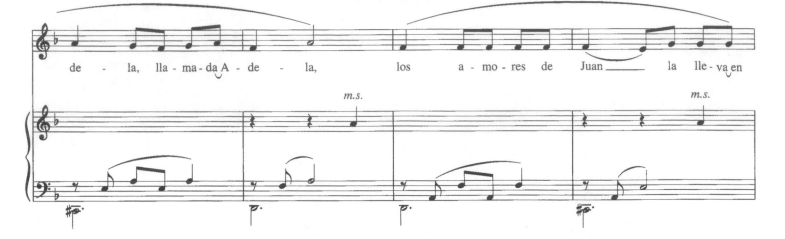

de - la, lla-ma-da A - de - la, los a - mo-res de Juan _____ la lle-va en

fer - ma, y e-lla sa - bí - a y e-lla sa - bí - a, que su a - mi - ga Do -

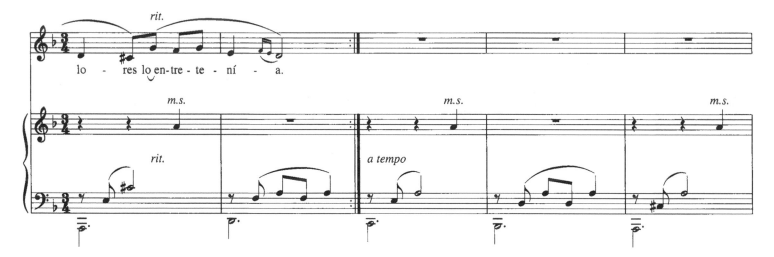

lo - res lo en-tre-te - ní - a.

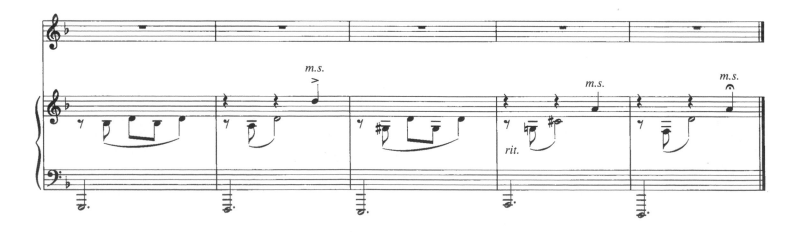

All Through the Night

This is the original Welsh text for the song:

Holl amrantau'r sêr ddywedant,
Ar hyd y nos,
"Dyma'r ffordd I fro gogoniant,"
Ar hyd y nos.
Golen arall yw tywyllwch,
I arddaug os gwir brydferthwch,
Teulu'r nef oedd mewn tawelwch,
Ar hyd y nos.

O mor siriol gwena seren,
Ar hyd y nos,
I oleno'i chwaerddaearen,
Ar hyd y nos.
Nos yw henaint pan ddaw cystudd,
Ond I harddu dyn a'i hwyrddydd,
Rho'wn ein golen gwan i'n gilydd,
Ar hyd y nos.

Since the Welsh language is unusual, and seldom spoken (even in Wales today), we did not include the original language text in the music. (Good luck trying to find someone to coach you in Welsh!)

"All Through the Night" is an anonymous folksong, meaning that we don't know who the composer was. It probably dates back at least to the 1700s. It has been arranged for voice and piano in this edition.

This song is a lullaby, and should be sung sensitively. In the second verse we realize that though the imagery of the song is of sleep, the song is actually about someone in the final sleep of death. The character of the person singing the song was deeply in love with someone who has died. He sings this tender lullaby at her graveside perhaps, which we can surmise from the line "Yet my strains of love shall hover, near the presence of my lover." We also learn that he is a minstrel who wanders the countryside, going from tavern to tavern, playing his Irish harp and singing. He is probably fairly young, and his beloved one died young, which we learn in the line "Love's young dream, alas! is over."

You should be aware that there have been several different versions of the English words to this song over the years. Another commonly heard version is a lullaby to a sleeping child. It's a sanitized approach, which takes away the darker emotions of the more authentic words presented in this edition.

All Through the Night

Welsh folksong
arranged by Nicholl

1. Sleep, my love, and peace at-tend thee, All through the night; Guard-ian an-gels God will lend thee,
2. Though I roam a min-strel lone-ly, All through the night; My true harp shall praise thee on-ly,

All through the night. Soft the drow-sy hours are creep-ing, Hill and vale in slum-ber steep-ing,
All through the night. Love's young dream, a - las! is o - ver, Yet my strains of love shall hov - er,

Love a-lone his watch is keep-ing, All through the night.
Near the pres-ence of my lov-er, All through the night.

Beautiful Dreamer

STEPHEN FOSTER (1826-1864)

Although he is hailed today as America's first popular song writer, Stephen Foster died a pauper. Born in Pennsylvania, Foster was largely a self-taught musician, though not an unsophisticated one. He consciously studied all the types of songs popular in the U.S. in the early 19th century (minstrel songs, German lieder, Irish songs, Scottish ballads, English folksongs, Italian opera arias, and African-American spirituals), and developed a personal style that synthesized all those types of song into a personal American style. Foster's father, wanting a steadier career than music for his son, sent him off to Cincinnati to work as an accountant. Foster eventually defied his father and supported himself with his music from 1850 until his death. Although he wrote some 200 songs, he never handled the business of music well. There were also few protections for a songwriter in America in his day. Copyright laws had not yet been well-developed nor legal precedents established to ensure a songwriter's material brought him income. Foster signed away rights to several of his songs, and wrote others on a minimal salary to meet his expenses. After his unhappy marriage dissolved, he moved to New York. Foster apparently was an alcoholic, and his life became out of control, struggling on the streets of the big city. He died in a strange accident. Dizzy from fever he fainted and struck his head on a stone. He had 38 cents in his pocket at his death, which was all the money he had in the world. Most of Foster's songs were tuneful and sentimental, and found a huge American audience. Such numbers as "My Old Kentucky Home," "Jeanie with the Light Brown Hair," and "Beautiful Dreamer," are still heard. In addition, he arranged some 30 minstrel songs, adding some "re-composition" of his own in songs such as "Oh! Susanna," "Camptown Races," and "Old Folks at Home." Foster also wrote a large number of hymns and Sunday school songs.

THOUGHTS ABOUT THE SONG ...

This is a tender serenade. Imagine that it is late at night. A young fellow is outside the window of his beloved. Everything is quiet. He sweetly sings for her to awaken to him. (He hopes she will come down into the yard and kiss him, of course.) This song should be sung sweetly and smoothly. This is no time for boisterous, loud singing. Take it easy. If you feel that the song is too short, you may perform it twice. If this is your choice, do not slow down at the end of the first verse. You might contrast the two verses by singing the second time more softly.

Beautiful Dreamer

words and music by
Stephen C. Foster

Flowing, in 3 (♩. = 1 beat)

Beau-ti-ful dream - er, wake un-to me Star-light and dew-drops are wait-ing for

thee._____ Sounds of the rude world heard in the day

Lulled by the moon-light have all passed a - way!

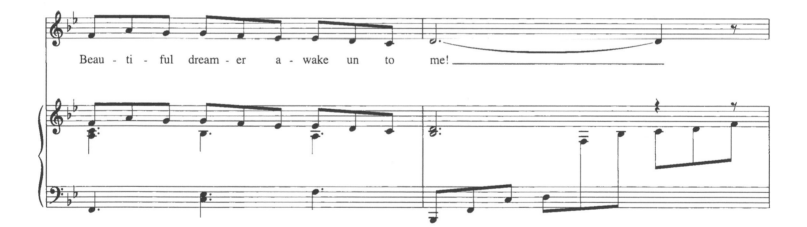

Alma del core

Alma del core, spirto dell'alma!	*Soul of my heart, spirit of my soul!*
sempre costante t'adorerò!	*always constant, you I will adore!*
Sarò contento nel mio tormento,	*I shall be content in my torment*
se quel bel labbro baciar potrò.	*if I will be able to kiss those beautiful lips.*

ANTONIO CALDARA (c. 1670-1736)
Italian cellist and composer Antonio Caldara composed an extraordinary amount of music over the course of his career. He completed 90 operas and sacred dramas, 43 oratorios, nearly 30 masses as well as other church music and chamber music. He was also a singer and was a competent performer on the violin and keyboard. Caldara spent the early years of his career in the court of the Duke of Mantua and Prince Ruspoli in Rome. In 1716 he landed the post of vice-conductor at the Viennese court. He found tremendous success there and in Salzburg, where many of his works were staged. When he died, in 1736, he was one of the most popular composers in Vienna. One of the most prolific composers of his era, the vast majority of his more than 3000 pieces were vocal works. Fluid melodies and rich harmonies were his trademark. He enjoyed musical jokes and would often use the musical form of a canon to create little plays on words, including jokes about of his own name (caldara means kettle in Italian).

THOUGHTS ABOUT THE SONG ...
"Alma del core" is an aria from a long forgotten opera *La costanza in amor vince l'inganno*. The style of opera at that time was comprised largely of formal solos (aria, pronounced **ah-**ree-ah), with little interaction between the characters, and often with little relation to the story. Except for some operas by Handel, the operas of this period (c 1650 until about 1775) are not in the modern repertoire. "Alma del core" is a spirited love song, fairly formal in its nature. You are singing to someone you adore, but the relationship is not yet where you want it to be. You say basically that you can endure the agony of longing and impatience if you can just hope to kiss your beloved in the future. The key to this kind of restrained, classical style is sincerity and beautiful singing. Refrain from extraneous hand motions. Communicate love and longing with your voice and your face. Most classical music is a stylized, contained expression of sincere, real emotion. You will need to study the Italian pronunciation lesson on the companion recording to become fluent in that language. We suggest that you speak the words many times before you ever sing them, and constantly compare your pronunciation with the recorded lesson. You might even ask a carefully selected friend to listen to your pronunciation as compared with the recorded Italian lesson.

PRONUNCIATION TIPS
Antonio [ahn-**tohn**-nee-oh] Caldara [kahl-**dah**-rah]

Alma del core

Anonymous Italian poem

music by
Antonio Caldara

Moderately (Minuet)

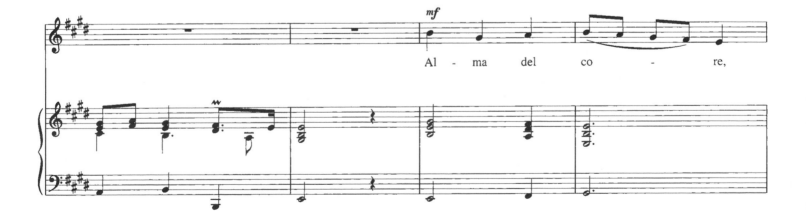

Al - ma del co - re,

spir - to ___ dell' ___ al - ma! ... Al - ma del

co - - re, spir - to ___ dell' ___ al - ma, sem - pre co - stan - te ___

t'a - do - re - rò, t'a - do - re - rò, t'a - - do - re -

rò, t'a - do - re - rò, t'a - - do - re - rò!

Al - ma del co - re, spir - to _ dell' _

al - ma, sem - pre co - stan - te _ t'a - do - re - rò,

sem - pre co - stan - te _ t'a - do - re - rò!

Sa - rò con - ten - to

nel mio tor - men - to, se quel bel lab - bro _____

ba - ciar _____ po - trò, se quel bel lab - bro, se quel bel

lab - bro _____ ba - ciar _____ po - trò.

Al - ma del co - re, spir - to _____ dell' _____ al - ma,

sem - pre co - stan - te _____ t'a - do - re - rò,

t'a - do - re - rò, t'a - do - re - rò,

t'a - do - re - rò, t'a - do - re - rò!

Al - ma del co - re, spir - to _____ dell' ____ al - ma,

sem - pre co - stan - te _____ t'a - do - re - rò,

sem - pre co - stan - te _____ t'a - do - re - rò.

poco rit.

Du bist wie eine Blume

Du bist wie eine Blume
so hold und schön und rein;
ich schau' dich an, und Wehmuth
schelicht mir in's Herz hinein.

You are like a flower
so charming and lovely and pure;
I look upon you, and sadness
creeps into my heart.

Mir ist, als ob ich die Hände
auf's Haupt dir legen sollt',
betend, dass Gott dich erhalte
so rein und schön und hold.

To me it is as if I my hands
should lay upon your head,
praying, that God keep you
so pure and lovely and charming.

ROBERT SCHUMANN (1810-1856)
The son of a German bookseller, composer Robert Schumann grew up loving both literature and music. He set out to become a great pianist, but problems with his hands put an end to that dream. He continued to compose however and, in 1834, founded the music journal *Neue Zeitschrift für Musik* in Leipzig, where he spent most of his adult life. Schumann proved to be an inspired critic who championed many important talents of the day, including a young Johannes Brahms. Robert fell in love with Clara Wieck, the daughter of his principal piano teacher. Clara, a fantastic pianist herself, performed widely throughout Europe at a time when women were rarely afforded such opportunities. In 1840, after overcoming endless hostile and serious objections from Clara's father, the two were married. The first few years of marriage were especially fruitful times for Schumann's composition of *Lieder* (literally meaning songs; the German term for art songs for voice and piano). Schumann's health began to fail in 1852. By 1854 he deteriorated to madness and was placed in an asylum where he died two years later. It was a tragic end to a great career. Schumann wrote over 300 songs, four symphonies and a great deal of piano and instrumental music. After Robert's death, Clara maintained a (probably platonic) lifelong friendship with composer Johannes Brahms. Although each professed a great love for the other, she refused to re-marry, out of respect for Schumann's memory. Heinrich Heine (1797-1856) was among the greatest of German poets, and a favorite of Schumann, who set 41 Heine poems to music. Heine's most characteristic work was the love poem, often times articulating the point of view of the unhappy lover.

THOUGHTS ABOUT THE SONG...
This is one of the most famous of all *Lieder*, or German art songs. The nineteenth century was a time of enormous activity for German art song composition (the setting of poetry to music for voice and piano). Many thousands of songs were written by major composers as well as many minor and lesser talents. The key to performing art song is in understanding the poetry. This poem by Heine, "Du bist wie eine Blume," is a very tender and sophisticated love poem. Interpretations may vary in all great art. Perhaps it is the poem of a young man in love with a young woman. Maybe he is just about to marry her, or it might be that the couple has just been married. Another interpretation might be that this is a poem of a father speaking to his daughter. As in much of the highest art, all the meanings are not spelled out, but implied. A rich subtext (the emotional context for the poem, though unstated) is possible in this poem. Work very carefully on the pronunciation of the words before you ever sing the poem. It's not just about being able to correctly pronounce isolated words with reasonable phonetic accuracy. You need to be able to express yourself fluently in this poem. That kind of fluency is your aim, even though you may not speak German. It may take several hours of work on speaking the words of the poem to feel completely confident about the song.

PRONUNCIATION TIPS
Robert Schumann [**shoo**-mahn]
Heinrich [**highn**-rick] Heine [**high**-nuh]

Du bist wie eine Blume

poem by
Heinrich Heine

music by
Robert Schumann

ein. Mir ist, _____ als ob ich die Hän _ de auf's

Haupt dir le - gen sollt', be - tend, dass Gott dich er -

hal te so rein und schön und hold.

Give a Man a Horse He Can Ride

GEOFFREY O'HARA (1882-1967)

Born in Ontario, Canada, composer Geoffrey O'Hara came to the United States in 1904, becoming a citizen in 1919. O'Hara was a performer as well as a composer. He appeared in vaudeville productions as a pianist, singer and actor as well as composing music for various productions. O'Hara served the U.S. Department of the Interior for a time as an instructor in American Indian music. He was a charter member of ASCAP (American Society of Composers, Authors and Publishers) in 1914. In addition to several operettas, O'Hara wrote some 300 songs. Several of his songs were extremely popular throughout the country, including "K-K-K-Katy," and "Give a Man a Horse He Can Ride." He composed the song "Your Eyes Have Told Me" for tenor Enrico Caruso. O'Hara died in 1967 in St. Petersburg, Florida.

THOUGHTS ABOUT THE SONG...

"Give a Man a Horse He Can Ride" is representative of the kind of song heard in operettas of the late nineteenth and early twentieth centuries. It's an exaggerated song of masculinity, so exaggerated, in fact, that it's funny. A performer would do well to realize this, and play the song for humor. O'Hara's song is very much rooted in the tradition of Gilbert & Sullivan operetta. Imagine a character in a costume of clothes from 1910, with a thick handle-bar mustache. It might even help you to imagine him on the stage of an old-fashioned theater. He smugly goes through all the things that make him self-content. You might try some strong stances and gestures for this particular number. Performing a song like this one is mostly about singing well and having a good time. (It's not so much about finding a vulnerable feeling inside you and in a stylized way communicating that to the audience, which is often what performing an art song can be about.) If you have the chance to hear or see a Gilbert & Sullivan operetta such *as HMS Pinafore, The Mikado* or *The Pirates of Penzance* (these are available in various performances on video), it will probably give you many strong ideas about how to present "Give a Man a Horse He Can Ride."

Give a Man a Horse He Can Ride

poem by
James Thomson

music by
Geoffrey O'Hara

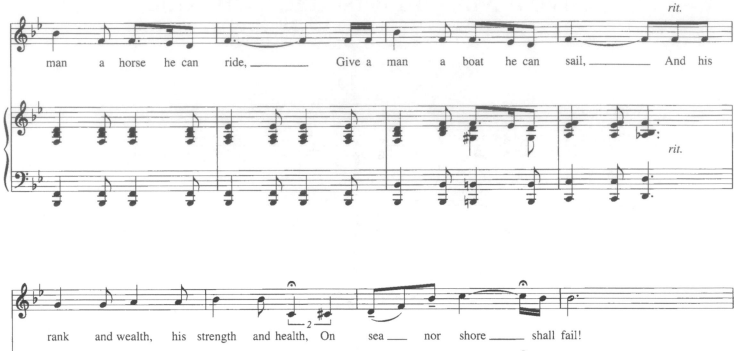

man a horse he can ride, _____ Give a man a boat he can sail, _____ And his

rank and wealth, his strength and health, On sea ___ nor shore _____ shall fail!

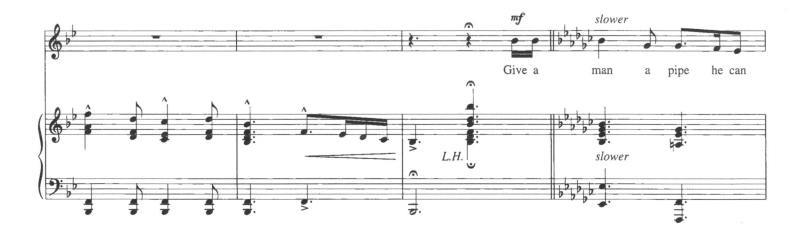

Give a man a pipe he can

smoke, _____ Give a man a book he can read _____ And his

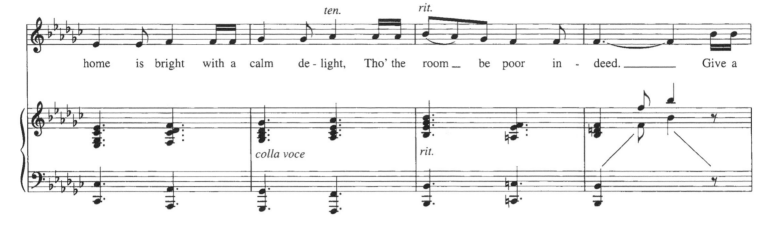

home is bright with a calm de-light, Tho' the room be poor in-deed. Give a

man a pipe he can smoke, Give a man a book he can read, And his

home is bright with a calm de-light, Tho' the room be poor in-deed. Give a

Expressivo *slower*

man a girl he can love, As I, oh my love, love

thee._____ And his heart is great, with the pulse of Fate, At home,_ on land, on

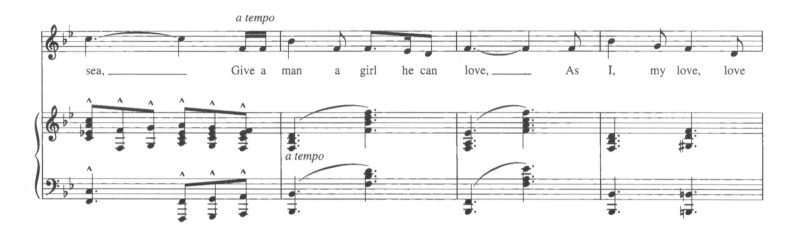

sea,_____ Give a man a girl he can love,_____ As I, my love, love

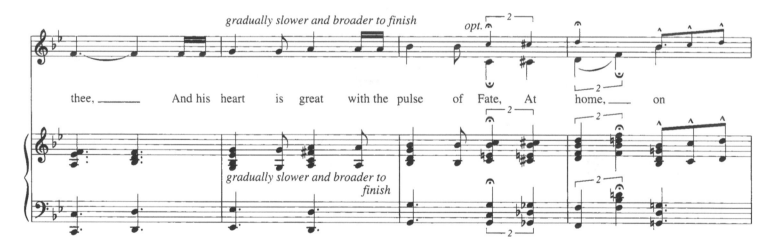

thee,_____ And his heart is great with the pulse of Fate, At home,_ on

land,_____ on sea!

The Sea

EDWARD MACDOWELL (1860-1908)

Edward MacDowell was the first American classical composer who was held in the same esteem, by his countrymen, as composers of European descent. He came of age in a time when America looked to Europe, particularly Germany, as the home of things cultural. MacDowell studied in Germany, eventually taking a teaching post in Darmstadt. He was secretly married in Darmstadt to one of his students, a pianist from Connecticut. The two had a public ceremony in the United States shortly thereafter. MacDowell was plagued by financial troubles in Germany and finally returned to America where he found that he and his works were held in the highest regard. He accepted an invitation from Columbia University to become its first professor of music, and had no trouble getting his works played by the major American orchestras. MacDowell resigned his Columbia position in 1904, a victim of university politics. The stress of the Columbia situation, a serious carriage accident, and a progressive illness pushed him into a deep depression which progressed into total insanity. In 1906 prominent American celebrities, including musicians and politicians, made a public request for donations to pay for his care. At his death (at age 47) $50,000 dollars was raised for the MacDowell Memorial Association. His widow, Marian Nevins MacDowell, later willed her husband's summer home to the same association. Located in Peterborough, Vermont, it became the MacDowell Colony, a retreat for American composers and writers. It is still a haven in which artists can work undisturbed, paying a minimal fee for food and lodging. William Dean Howells was a prominent literary figure of his time, principally known for being the editor of *The Atlantic Monthly* and *Harper's*. His poetry, as in "The Sea," was a minor part of his published work.

THOUGHTS ABOUT THE SONG ...

This is a wonderfully dark song about a sailor lost at sea. It begins "one sails away to sea," meaning the sailor, and "one stands on the shore and cries," meaning his wife or sweetheart left behind. The ship sinks. The woman waits for many years without a word, while her loved one lies dead in his "coral bed." It's a very vivid little song, and if you are a good storyteller as well as a singer, you can paint a strong sequence of images with your voice and communication: the wife left on shore, teary-eyed and waving to her sailor husband on ship; the stormy crash of the ship and the consequent drowning death to all aboard; the steadfast woman on shore waiting and weeping and filled with worry and dread; and the sailor's dead body at the bottom of the sea. The more clearly you can imagine each of these scenes in succession, and feel the emotions of each, the more compelling your performance will be. Experiment with different vocal colors to express the story.

The Sea

poem by
William Dean Howells

music by
Edward MacDowell

in vain, Man _ y and man _ y a year. _____ But the state _ ly wide _ winged

ship lies wrecked, Lies wrecked on the un - known deep; _____ Far un - der, dead in his

cor - al bed, The lov - er lies a - sleep, _____ Far un - der, dead in his

cor - al bed The lov - er lies a - sleep, _____ a - sleep. _____

O cessate di piagarmi

O cessate di piagarmi,	*Oh, stop wounding me,*
o lasciatemi morir,	*oh, let me die,*
luc'ingrate, dispietate,	*ungrateful eyes, pitiless,*
più del gelo e più del marmi	*more than ice and more than stone*
fredde e sorde a' miei martir.	*cruel, and deaf to my suffering.*

ALESSANDRO SCARLATTI (1660-1725)

Scarlatti's life story is filled with legendary stories of personal and polictal entanglements and curious back-room dealings. The Italian composer came from a family of musicians. His two sisters were both prominent singers in Naples. It has been alleged that they finagled jobs for both Alessandro and their brother Francesco, a violinist. Whatever the case, Alessandro was made maestro di cappella and Francesco was hired as first violinist in the Naples court orchestra at the same time. Brother Tommaso was tenor who also made his career in Naples. Scarlatti's son Pietro Filippo was an organist and composer, and son Domenico was a brilliant keyboard player and composer. Scarlatti wrote some 115 operas, although only about 70 of them have survived. Once thought to have been the founder of the Neapolitan school of opera, he is now believed to have been more of a participant than an innovator. Scarlatti was remarkably adaptable throughout his career, moving from opera to oratorio and cantata writing following a ban on opera performance. He composed over 700 secular cantatas and 35 oratorios as well as ten masses and a wealth of other liturgical music.

THOUGHTS ABOUT THE SONG...

This solo is a well-known aria from a long forgotten opera entitled *Pompeo* (1683). Though it doesn't explicitly tells us so, we can assume that this is a song sung by a jilted lover. The woman he loves with all his heart doesn't love him anymore. More than that, perhaps she is downright hostile to him. Why doesn't the suffering lover simply avoid her? We can conjecture about that. Perhaps he has no choice because of his professional or social obligations. Or maybe he loves her so much that he can't bear to be away from her presence, even though she seems to detest him. This is as sad and poignant a love song as you will find in any language. Besides emotional pain, mixed with love, the song also has a restless longing about it, longing either for peace or for her love. The song requires some expressive finesse. You may try the second verse softer than the first. Be certain to fully acquaint yourself with the Italian words. Listen to the recorded pronunciation lesson over and over, repeating the words many times until you feel completely correct, comfortable and fluent. This may take several hours of work. At the point of performance you want to focus on singing beautifully and expressing sincere emotion, not on self-consciously trying to pronounce the Italian diction correctly. That should be completely under control long before the performance.

PRONUNCIATION TIP

Alessandro [ah-lehs-**sahn**-droh] Scarlatti [scahr-**laht**-tee]

O cessate di piagarmi

words by
Nicola Minato

music by
Alessandro Scarlatti

The Slighted Swain

This is an anonymous song of the 1600s from England. We simply don't know who the composer was. The original composition, common in this period, was in a style called figured bass. Most likely the composer's score was a melody with the words, and under it a bass line, with the harmony noted under each note of the bass line. Players of that period would then "realize" or improvise harmony as indicated over the composed bass line. This edition is a realization arranged for voice and piano.

"Swain" is a old word (rooted in Middle English) meaning a country youth, probably a shepherd or a peasant. So a "slighted swain" would be a country youth who has been jilted by his lover, who in this case is Chloe. The text is typical of an English love poem of this period. It may help you to think about what the song means to see the words presented away from the music.

Chloe proves false, but still she is charming;
Nature, like beauty, her temper has made
Subject to change; o'er each heart she will range,
Always the fairest, ever the rarest,
Always the fairest in beauty arrayed.

Banish my senses, but let her not slight me,
Love ne'er was made to inherit disdain;
Love is a bubble that gives mankind trouble,
Ever alluring, seldom enduring,
Chloe who flouts me I sigh for in vain.

Apparently, at least according to the character who is singing the song, the beautiful Chloe [pronounced **kloh**-ee] is quite a flirt, and charms many men, though she is true to none of them. We hear that she "flouts" him, which means scorns him, and he pines away for her even though he knows he has no hope of ever marrying her. His unreturned love for her has made him bitter, understandably.

It's a lively song, which illustrates his active internal emotions. This fellow is not one to mope around and weep about being rejected. He's more the type to vent his feelings in a manner that is closer to anger than any other emotion.

You will do well to execute the rhythm cleanly, which will give the song the animation it needs. Also, because it is such a British text and musical style, work hard at achieving a light (not overdone) English accent for singing this song. One specific tip is to roll the R's in a way that is not done in American English, in words such as "proves," "fairest," and "arrayed." But in other contexts, minimize the R sound in a British style, such as in "charming" (which should sound more like "chahming"), or "temper" (which should sound more like "tempuh"). British diction is also more energetic and annuciated than American English. One warning though: a bad British accent is a very obvious sign of a bad actor or singer. Make sure you thoroughly prepare the British diction over many practice sessions.

The Slighted Swain

17th century English song
arranged by H. Lane Wilson

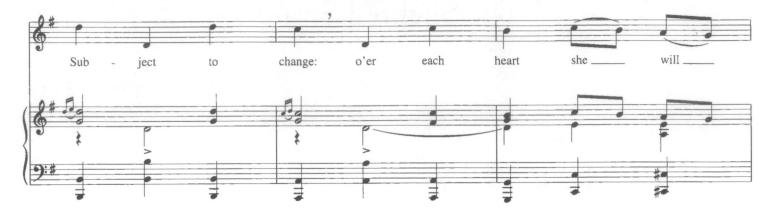

Sub - ject to change: o'er each heart she ___ will ___

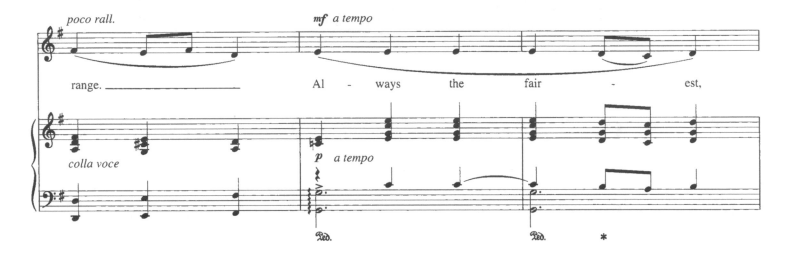

poco rall.　　　　　　mf a tempo

range. ___ Al - ways the fair - est,

colla voce　　　　　p a tempo

p

ev - er the rar - est, Al - ways the

p　　　　　　　　　　　　f

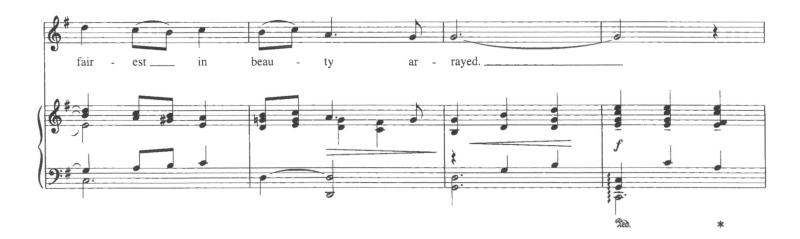

fair - est ___ in beau - ty ar - rayed. ___

f

f   *p*

Ban - ish my sen - ses, but let her not slight _____ me,

mf   *p*

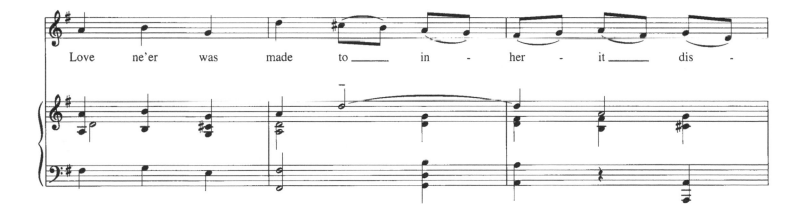

Love ne'er was made to ___ in - her - it ___ dis -

dain;   Love is a bub - ble that gives man - kind ___

p

Ped.   Ped.

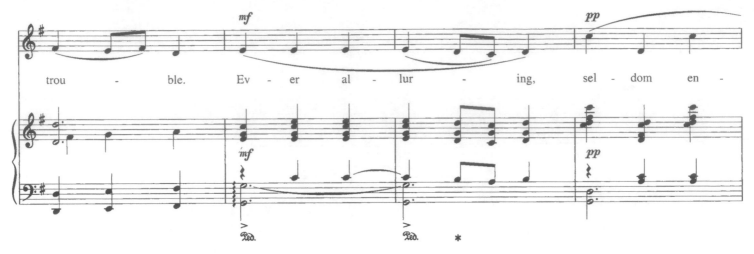

trou - ble. Ev - er al - lur - ing, sel - dom en -

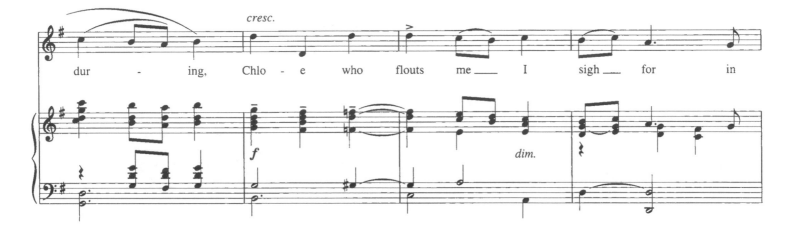

dur - ing, Chlo - e who flouts me ___ I sigh ___ for in

vain, _____ Chlo - e who flouts me ___ I sigh ___ for in

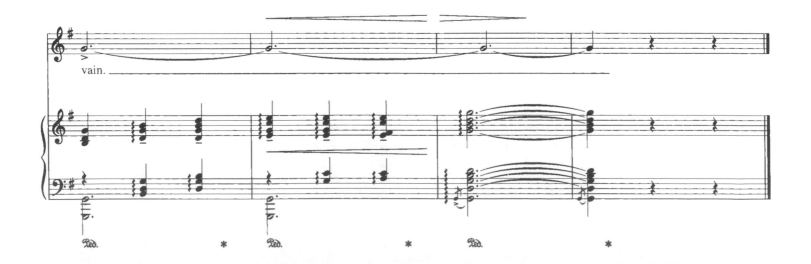

vain. _____

Swing Low, Sweet Chariot

HARRY T. BURLEIGH (1866-1949)

African-American composer and arranger Harry Thacker Burleigh was born in Erie, Pennsylvania in 1866, one year after the end of the Civil War. His grandfather had been a slave who was "let go" by his slaveholders when he became blind. Upon graduating from high school, Burleigh won a scholarship to study at the National Conservatory of Music in New York, and was able to make the move with the help of many donations from contributors in his home town of Erie. While at the conservatory he was heavily influenced by the school's director, composer and conductor Antonín Dvorák. Like many musicians, Burleigh found it difficult to make a living performing and composing. His principal employment throughout most of his adult life was as a music editor at the New York office of the Italian music publisher Ricordi. He spent his summers traveling to Milan to work at the home office. Burleigh composed some 265 vocal pieces, and is credited with a collection of African-American minstrel melodies. He was a prominent baritone soloist in New York, first at St. George's Church, then for 25 years at Temple Emanuel-El. Burleigh also regulary sang in recital. He did ground-breaking work with his documentation and arrangements of 187 spirituals for choir. Burleigh was also one of the first to take this music of African-American heritage into the concert hall in arrangements for solo voice and piano. He had learned many spirituals as a child, listening to his grandfather sing. Burleigh was an excellent and respected vocal coach who worked with famous singers such as Enrico Caruso, Marian Anderson and Paul Robeson. He was a founding member of ASCAP. Among the honors bestowed on Harry Burleigh were an honorary master's degree from Atlanta University, an honorary Doctor of Music degree from Harvard University, and in 1917 the Spingarn Medal was awarded to him by the N.A.A.C.P., citing him for the highest achievement by an African-American for the year 1916.

THOUGHTS ABOUT THE SONG ...

Spirituals, predominantly the songs of African-American slaves, are an important part of our American musical heritage. Though they have their roots with African-Americans, experts on spirituals maintain that today they are music for all singers of all races. "Swing Low, Sweet Chariot" illustrates a point of view common to many spirituals: the sadness and longing of a people confined against their will, and a faith in God and in heaven ("home" in the words of the song), the ultimate reward and escape from a hard life of misery. Heaven was the only hope and escape for most of these people. A singer may use as much dialect in pronunciation of the words as is comfortable for this style of spiritual. Some singers will feel perfectly comfortable using a full-fledged southern African-American dialect. Others will feel more comfortable staying more closely to standard American English pronunciation. This is a slow, sustained song that will require excellent breath control for the long phrases. Sometimes the songs the slaves sang helped to make the work seem lighter. One can easily imagine a group of field workers, swinging sickles in a slow rhythmic way as they sang "Swing Low, Sweet Chariot."

PRONUNCIATION TIP

Burleigh [**burr**-lee]

Swing Low, Sweet Chariot

African-American Spiritual
arranged by Harry T. Burleigh

look'd o - ver Jor - dan, what did I see,_ Com-in' for to car-ry me home?_ A band_ of an - gels

com-in' af - ter me,_ Com-in' for to car-ry me home. Swing low, sweet char - i - ot,_

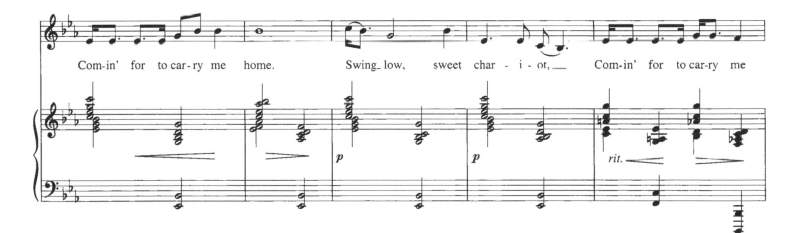

Com-in' for to car-ry me home. Swing_ low, sweet char - i - ot,_ Com-in' for to car-ry me

home._